Rogue Waves

Rogue Waves

Alan Birkelbach

Texas Review Press
Huntsville, Texas

FIRST EDITION, 2011
Requests for permission to reproduce material from this work should be
sent to:

Permissions
Texas Review Press
English Department
Sam Houston State University
Huntsville, TX 77341-2146

Acknowledgements:

Some of these poems first appeared in Texas Review, Windhover, Voices
de la Luna, and the Austin Poetry Society Anthology 2009.

The cover artwork, by Hokusai, is entitled The Great Wave off Kanagawa.
Cover design is by Nancy Parsons of Graphic Design Group.

Library of Congress Cataloging-in-Publication Data

Birkelbach, Alan.
   Rogue waves / Alan Birkelbach. -- 1st ed.
      p. cm.
   ISBN 978-1-933896-48-9 (pbk. : alk. paper)
   I. Title.
   PS3552.I7543R64 2011
   811'.54--dc22
                              2010039748

Dedication

If there is such a thing as a Muse
then this book is for her,
for giving me the idea whole and intact,
all at once, in a hurry.

And, of course, as always—to Laura

Table of Contents

Rogue Waves

THE CANOE CAUGHT UNAWARES

We think our lives smooth basins,
glassy as summer rivers,
placid as captured lakes.
We assign actuarials to random events:
lightning strikes, falling satellites,
Jesus coming back.

It takes a disturbance,
a lurch, a wobble.
Maybe an accidental meeting,
a brushing of hands,
a closeness that lingers
and then emerges later, deeper, larger
in an unrelated conversation.

Maybe it's a baby kicking a bathtub,
the waves conspiring around the rubber duck.
Maybe a bird bathes in a random puddle
and blesses your car with splash.
Maybe a current remains from a dammed spillway
and journeys over submerged abandoned bicycles,
piles of mossy old tires, scoured Indian points.

It can turn into a question to which
we cannot accept the answer:

to walk the dock, the wind barely kissing our cheek,
only to find our canoe submerged
and sitting on the bottom, looking up,
its rope barely rustling on the steps,
the thwarts holding its mouth open
in permanent surprise.

TYPEFACE

This poem is set in a typeface
called Apocryphal Hominid 10 point.
Its curlicues and unexpected angles
may be confusing.
It may seem as if
you have been submerged in lines
or reduced to mere symbols.
You may begin to think too much about the presentations
and too little about what they represent.
As if when you see a beautiful woman on the street
and your mind begins to wander.
You might imagine yourself walking beside her.
You might call her Estrella
and she might call you *mi roble, mi momento.*
She will have a slightly chubby bottom,
heels half an inch too tall.
In 1611 a slightly deranged monk
had too much wine and found a way
to codify both pleasures of the flesh
and a rather horrific cataclysm in
marginal letter-endings and stylized curls.
It was a secret all about sound and image
and, especially, symbol congruency, easily
translatable once you knew the key.
Mi momento. No tree lives forever,
not even Yggdrasil. You will want Estrella
to choose what you will do, as if she will know.
You will want her to know.
She will unlatch the watch from your wrist,
and say it is all about the sounds
that will happen next.

THE HARDY-WEINBERG LAW

*The Hardy-Weinberg principle states that genetic
frequencies in a population remain constant from
generation to generation unless outside influences are
introduced. In nature these outside influences are always
in effect. Therefore, the Hardy-Weinberg principle is an
ideal condition that can never be achieved.*

If Columbus and La Salle
had not sailed until
their sails were perfectly ironed
then today we might
be working for the Aztecs.

Some poets will not submit their poems
for public consumption
until the lines are exactly right.
Their notebooks end up
bulging with cabochons.

It's the messiness of things
that makes them perfect:
the sugar falling
from the cinnamon roll,
the ice cream melting in the cone.

Flood waters rise
and kiss against doorways.
The fire comes
down the mountain.
The wind pushes trees into yards.

When I was much younger
I wrote the characteristics
of my perfect girl

on a piece of paper,
did a little chant,

then burned the list in a coffee can,
sending my wishes to the universe.
Now you are sleeping in the crook of my arm,
and maybe you are drooling a little,
and definitely snoring,

and I am thankful for all bugs
that will ever land in my coffee,
grateful for all nails
that will ever make my tires
breathless.

BRONTOSCOPY

*The ancient art of divination by listening
to the sound of thunder.*

Thunder on Thursday is a good omen
although I think this might border on phrenology
and what I have bumped into recently.
Perhaps if we didn't already have Madame Cleo and
Oprah and Facebook
then we would spend more time
looking for signs ourselves
and less time expecting directions.

In a small town in Mexico
someone, in the midst of remodeling,
found an image in the vague shape
Of Our Lady of Guadalupe
in their sheetrock. It was never questioned
why Our Lady was hiding
beneath old wallpaper.
Instead, the story centered
on how all the candelarias
had flown off the shelves of the local markets,
regardless of whether the saints
were applicable or not.
People wrapped themselves
in candlewicks of holiness
in case drywall had the ability to foreshadow.

It was as if all the kids
in grade school in the Roman era
were given the assignment of
"Go home tonight and create a divining system.
And remember this will count toward

one-quarter of your final grade."
Some less bright kids counted chicken eggs,
some referenced Delphi,
some counted Grandma's aches and pains,
and some actually looked truly outward
trying to comprehend a larger measuring thing.
They might have understood
they were wrapped in holiness every day,
in every dark storm,
if they would just light a candle,
and listen.

WHEN ALEXANDER THE GREAT'S MOM HAD
HIS PHOTO DONE AT SEARS

She constantly chided him.
"Don't fidget. Stand up straight.
What will the Persians think?"
She had a coupon so she wanted to try him
in as many outfits as possible.
He was always so dour, even posturing;
far too grim for a five-year old.
But he was no more grim than she was smart:
she was going to take advantage of this phase,
the tilting of his head,
the puffing of his infantile chest.
Of course, he did keep talking in the
        third person
and that bothered her some.
"Alexander does not like this background.
These shoes pinch Alexander's feet.
Alexander will comb his own hair."
And when the bow tie came up he simply said,
"I would not be Alexander."—and refused to put it on.
He tried the cowboy outfit, under duress,
sitting astride a wooden horse
(which still bore the 'Made in Thessaly' label—
she could have died.)
He seemed relatively comfortable—
but kept calling the conchos 'girl's baubles'.
When he tried on the tiny pin-stripe suit
he only quit scowling when he realized
the matching tie had a picture of Aristotle.
It was when she relented, finally,
and allowed him to stand, bare-chested,
one foot propped up on a carpeted step,
a fist clenched and close to his body,

the other arm extended like a spear,
that she dared followed his eyes
that were looking through,
and past, the cameraman,
and for a chilling, pride-filled second
she believed, as only a parent can believe,
that he could crush the world
beneath those sandaled, dimpled feet.

¡Mis Amoebas!

This child's toy should have
better enunciation.

It's as if God said, "Let there be Light"
and the second vice-president
he was shouting the command to
across the galaxy heard instead "Let there Delight!"
and he ended up just shrugging his cosmic shoulders
and re-interpreting the command
to suit his own agenda.

And chicken lips. We should never pay attention
to overheard conversations while we stand in line
for street lights.
From then on we can only imagine
pullets pulling on cheap cigarettes,
a brim pulled low over one eye,
a feathery Sidney Greenstreet in the background.

In college sheer plod made plow down sillion shine—
but a telemarketer from Ceylon
interrupting me at dinner
can turn it into mere wad make billion
faster than I can hang up.

Sometimes the syllables come out cleanly
and we only mis-hear.
But sometimes the words are as thick
as slow, muddy water over mossy boulders.
It seems like it might be a language we know
if only the sending lips would form it correctly.

So I am left with this lingering image

that haunts me at the most gay of times:
An innocent Hispanic girl,
with a mouthful of rocks,
thinking only in the moment,
as she blithely leads a herd
of giant, one-celled organisms
to a tacqueria, a fiesta,
or some strange and wonderfully bizarre quinciñera.

Famous Poets Trading Cards

These are the small packets
snuggled with slabs of gum
you will never find.

"I'll trade you two Robert Frosts,"
(who is rather common), "for a Rilke
or an Auden."
You can't give away your Wordsworths
but your Shakerley Marmions
and Stephen Ducks are like gold
(even if no one knows who they are).
You always treat your Amy Lowells
and Emily Dickinsons with respect;
you have no trouble at all sticking
Carl Sandburg in the spokes of your bike.
Then there are the team cards
(the post modernists, the beats,
the romantics, etcetera):
The faces are so tiny and you never really believe
Li Po wore his baseball hat backwards.
Of course, every card
has a library of information on the back:
how many double dactyls they wrote,
their sonnet sequences, their favorite topics,
their count of books published, their Nobels won—
all their metrical runs batted in,
how much they tinkered with classical forms,
how many times they rhymed Heavens to Dale Evans,
how often they alluded to
the connotations of chance.

DEAR YOURS TRULY MY LOVE

My beloved tax collector—
as you can see you are special to me.
Have I not written you checks larger,
and more painful,
than alimony for year after year?
My special, my one and only.
Yours truly.
Salutations can be as meaningless as saying
that something is On Sale!
Or the deal is Once in a Lifetime!
The woman says "You will never know
any one like me again!"
That is, of course, correct if you
totally accept that something must be
A and Not A to be true.
When you have washed
your Grateful Dead t-shirt over and over,
and it's thirty years since the last concert you went to,
you've finally noticed that the black thread,
blood, and skeleton
have all faded and washed into gray
and Easter-bunny pink.
You give in one morning,
shrug the way your father used to,
and you use that shirt to wash your car.
It's the same shirt—but you're not the same man.
Nobody cares but you
how many times you wear a pair of socks,
how many times you get married,
how many times you give up smoking.
Your closure is your own, as many times
as you want to use it. Say it again:
Tell me the story of how you ran into Marilyn Monroe

at the bus depot
and how she called you "Honey"
and how it changed your life,
how you're sure she meant it just for you
no matter how many times she had said it before.

GASPING

They haunt you afterwards
when you discover they aren't rhetorical
or aren't solved with a simple
yes or no.

Paper or plastic?
What does this red button do?
What political party are you?
Left or right? Regular or unleaded?
Are you married?
Cream or no cream?

Mostly you can stumble through,
flail around, claim lack of sleep, distraction,
change the subject.
You hit yourself in the head later
when you come up with the clever answer,
but once your mind is prone to disengage
then that gear tooth is broken.

For instance,
one day your wife asks
"Does this dress make me look fat?"
and your cognitive functions
are left standing in neutral,
spinning like crazy but generating no sparks.

Shrugging and grunting won't do,
you can't caveat,
and "I don't know" is absolutely the worst.

It's like being alone on a skiff
and hearing the clacking

of chitinous nails against the boat side,
a mossy hand on the gunwale,
the sibilant, burbly hiss of air
drawn over gills and larynx
not used to human speech.

Maybe it will be the moss draped like a boa,
or the way the color of her eyes
shifts constantly from blue to green.

It could be any of that,
as her eyes will lock yours,
but more likely it will be that
she will ask the question
she has asked countless sailors before.
She will wait,
then swim in closer in her serrated impatience,
this time grabbing the oar,
and ask just one more time,
"Is Alexander the King alive?"

AS MARTIN LUTHER WALKED
ALONG THE ROAD ONE DAY

his best friend beside him was struck by lightning.
Naturally, the whole 'Sal to Tarsus'
thing came to mind
and, sure enough,
Martin immediately turned it into a sign.
He never seemed to question
why his friend was the target;
he just immediately
made the event about himself.

I know a man who gave his wife a hammer
for her birthday
because one day he had seen her lift
a cookie sheet of cookies hot from the oven
with one big, mittened hand
and he thought she might appreciate
something else that was practical
and had such good balance.
As certain as steps on a ladder
he felt he owned a piece
of the holiness
of personal equilibrium.

When you drive past
small, frame churches on rural roads
there is always a lawn for after-service discussion,
a gravel parking lot, a swing-set painted red,
and a sign in front, usually painted white as a lamb
with big black letters.
And on that sign you can expect to see
hours of worship, maybe an alert about a revival,
some quote from Corinthians at the very least.

But on one particular sign it reads:
"We Kill Fire Ants".

You will not be a mile down the road
before you will begin to feel
a vague, unreachable itch.

Rogue Waves

The slight tremors
create ripples in your coffee
and belie impending trouble underneath

We're doomed, of course,
so why does it catch us by surprise?

The car has leapt the curb
and we still insist on spending a moment
in contemplation.

It's like watching the re-enactment of Krakatoa
over and over, the slow-motion replay,
the rocks spraying out,
the ocean rising,
the villagers looking up from the net-mending.

We think ourselves omniscient,
calculate angles,
create quick metaphors in our head,
search for buoys to grasp like a faith.
We try to ground ourselves in questions.
"Why here and not over there?"

There's no divining.
Scientists can only guess.
The dogs won't bark
and the cattle won't stampede.
Even John the Baptist and Nostradamus
would have to scramble.

Some moments don't leave time for questions.
Not like stacking stone blocks

and you pull the bottom one out.
Even a slave could see that grief coming.

This is that piece of debris from the sky
smashing through your roof and into the recliner
where you just told your husband to sit
but he wasn't yet because he couldn't find
the remote. As the upholstery smolders
you both immediately start rewinding
past prayers in your head.

This is the windborne trash
that clings to your windshield
and blinds you in the rain.

This is being in line at the bank on hold-up day.

This is being swept along
on a ley-line of circumstance,
one event angling off another,
an airborne twig shearing
the final thread that was holding the
sword you did not know was there.

This is the keystone that dislodges,
the chain that breaks, the distracted wasp,
the mountain lion out of range,
the intercepted letter.

This is God tripping on a phantom stone
and using you to break his fall.

To Every Social Studies Teacher

Here is the poem you cannot
pass on to the junior high students.
They are still trying
to get their heads around Flanders Field.
Now Pasternak eludes both them and Russia.
And good luck dealing with the school board
regarding that Ginsberg thing.

Social Studies is all about
believing in the temporal intimacy of a moment.
Like those unguarded sentences
your mother told you when you were five.
She was sipping her coffee
and didn't really seem to be talking to you.
She was talking about that man,
The Marlboro Man,
that man who was thick as a tree,
and inscrutable as Joyce.
That man who was handled and tooled.
That man who would look at you and say
you could give him any name you wanted.
That man who would wake up before you,
cook your favorite eggs,
then bring them back to bed
and feed you both with just one fork.

Choking Ahogo

Poor Ahogo.
Someone has put up a sign
on how to end him.
It seems amazing no one has caught him yet.
Based on these instructions
it does not seem as if he will put up
much of a struggle.
He must be relatively famous
if he is only known by his first name.
"Hey! Ahogo! We told you
your jay-walking would get you in trouble!"

Certainly Miss Daisy needed driving,
and records indicate that Cain was raised,
(and I have heard that members of the Fit family
are not opposed to being tossed),
but I suspect you will not find
a sign in a post office or grocery store
that instructs you on how
to Free Gratis or Poison Sumac.

No one else is paying attention to this sign.
I will forget it too
and hope Ahogo never crosses my path.
Let Fate grant him the same invulnerability
as his wildly gyrating cousin
Slippery Cuidado.

STRONG BONES

Now that he's grown
he might still be searching
the cosmos for it,
blue x-ray eyes
peering into every corner.

True to its origin
It must have been
set on its own
extended journey
from the faraway planet
called Kansas,
propelled like a orphaned rocket
from Fate's launch pad.

How could little Clark
have lost this?
Maybe he sat it down
absentmindedly
when he heard a far-off kitten
mewing for help.
Maybe he got distracted
by the infinite microscopic universe
of a very earthly grain of wheat.

This would not have been a thing
he would have abandoned lightly.
Destiny might just have set it rolling
along a dusty road,
then into hands which might, or might not,
have been villainous.

Regardless,
now Superman's lost thermos
sits quietly on the shelf
of this thrift store,
its insignia throbbing
gently in the dark.
It waits, in its alien way,
to again keep milk cold forever,
its metallic skin
perfectly
unbroken,
undented,
unscratched.

Jesus Stopped By and Fixed My Grill

Jesus stopped by today
and raised my grill from the dead.
It made me question the whole
divine spark of life issue.
I started mourning for all the toasters
I might have tossed too soon.
And blenders. And piece of junk lawnmowers.
Maybe they could have been reclaimed.

I can't honestly say the parts on my grill
look new. I mean, consider
that it's not as if the people
he raised from the dead
came back as babies after all.
It wasn't a do-over, a start-again at go.
And no one was made immortal.
No, it was only a pause, a deferral,
a holding off of the imperial inevitable.

My grill just works now. It's still rusty.
The shelves are loose. But it fires up.
I offered Jesus a beer in thanks,
if he had a minute,
but he smiled and declined,
said he was on his way to some
carburetor a few blocks over.
I shook his hand, turned up the flame,
torn open the franks,

just like Lazarus must have done
after all the hosannas and news-spreading
and re-tellings.

I'm betting he ran off
somewhere privately with his wife
checking to see what parts still worked.

The Pipes of Pan

When we,
quite by chance,
ended up standing
side by side
watching some
delicious nymph
bounce her bosom
down the street,
with only an acknowledging
nod of our heads
we both knew
that on him
immortality
had been
misspent.
He was as shaggy
as a derelict Hasidic
and he leaned
on a worn and gnawed
cane.
He put his shoulder
against a light-post
and started beating
on his crotch
with his stick.
He looked up at me,
shook his head,
and shrugged his shoulders
as if to say nothing, nothing.
He pointed me up street.
He turned the other way.

TIME BOUNDED

Sometimes it's all about how
curiosity drives our steps
and how we set our goals.
How might things have changed
if the Mayans had sailed east?
Of course, the Europeans
already had a continuity
and were pretty sure their
empire and arts habits
had carved their place in history.
They might not have been able
to grasp it when the Mayans said,
"Don't worry.
Look past these turquoise amulets and jade knives.
We're not really into
the whole conquering thing.
Oh sure, there's some tribal disagreements
but we'll keep them in our backyard.
You've got some mighty fine buildings here.
Just keep doing what you're doing.
We just came over to let you know
that we've done some checking and,
well, there's an expiration date coming up
and you might want to do some planning.
Now, we gotta go. Long voyage home and all that."
How many fair-skinned people
standing there on the pier
would be waving farewell to the harbingers,
their brows furrowed, debating whether to believe,
deciding to pay more attention
to all stops on the way back home.

Tinkerbell In Trousers

Mighty Mouse,
Steve Canyon,
Buck Rodgers.
We want these to be temporary.
We do not want them to have back-stories.
We do not want them to like blackjack,
or have appeared on Jerry Springer,
We don't want to see their baby pictures.
We don't want to meet their children.
We don't want to watch
the Justice League grow old.
We don't want to read how
Tinkerbell has lesbian tendencies.
We want them all to be in and out and done,
as temporal as ourselves,
as complete and perfect as Christmas gifts.
We don't want to know
where the boxes came from
or where they go.
We don't want to know
what powers or drives our fantasies.
We just want to see them fly.

DELEGATION

Sometimes delegation just won't do
and it's all about performing the task yourself.
Like in the middle of the night
when Persephone pushes Pluto out of bed
with her insistent (and guilt-inducing) toe
and says Get Up, Get Up, I think I heard
a noise out there close to Rome,
maybe Athens. So he rolls out of bed,
climbs in the chariot,
and does a cursory drive around all the stalagmites
(he even has Cerberus growl into the darkness).
But if Persephone still hears the noise
she's not going to like his answer
until she checks things herself,
her bunny slippers glowing like spring
down the stone hallways.

You hand the task off
and the message gets garbled.
Rosencrantz and Guildenstern end up
vacationing in Sweden,
or someone shows up with
a lock of Grendel's hair instead of his arm.
It just leads to more trouble.
It lengthens the process.

You pay to have a secure stone wall built
but afterwards you discover holes so large
Pyramus and Thisbe could have
crawled through them
and started a family.

Sometimes you wish you were the person
in charge of calendars and watches.
But alas, that job has been delegated already.
You have looked in the mirror in the mornings
and been surprised,
and reach the conclusion that man
is doing a poor job,
letting things burn through so quickly.

Those old gods, you decide, must be
given special dispensation,
near the top of the decision tree,
never getting older,
given enough authority
to frighten or satisfy mortals,
but not necessarily
other gods.

WHY BEING FIFTY-PLUS IS THE BEST AGE

There are always at least
four older people in horror movies:
two that die early because they don't believe
that a spider as big as a tractor
was running across their yard,
and two that die next-to-last
trying to protect their grandkids
from the rampaging mummy.
(There's always an alpha teenage couple left alive
for sequels.)

It's best to always believe
in the extrapolated unreality of things.
You learn to duck, be fast on the draw,
be able to tango on command.
You learn to cope, accept the scars,
bend a branch, leave a sign.

Maybe, after your adventures,
you write your memoirs.
Maybe you write a list:

"Being Fifty Plus Is the Best Age
because all but the slowest dinosaurs are extinct;
because we got those pyramid thingies built;
because we survived the Black Plague;
because I painted her name onto a stone, there,
right there,
along the river. "Ooaug".
Well, maybe I didn't use those exact letters,
the Phoenicians haven't come along yet
so the whole symbolic thing hasn't gelled.

My mark for her is more like an auk or a deer.
I'm sure she'll know herself when she sees herself."

No geologic plate is ever stable.
Earthquakes lift and reefs are exposed
and pretty soon there's an island
complete with natives that want independence.
They start keeping track of history,
honoring elders,
always listening to hear
if the ground will shift again.

And here we are, listening to Elvis
(the best music EVER)
spreading out our picnic
on the stones of the river bed.
We accept that around that corner
there might be a meteorite
that might contain an omnivorous alien.
But until he shows up
I am going to scratch your name
on this rock and this rock and this rock
and set them in the river
so the water,
through the minutes, hours, and years,
will say your name again and again
and every time you hear it
you will know it's you, it's you.

HIS NEXT TASK

After Michael told the Virgin Mary
the glorious news
he returned to heaven to,
"Well Done, Faithful Servant",
a slew of seraphamic high-fives,
and an unending chorus of,
"Who's the Angel?"

But it's the problem with any plan
be it five year or five eons.
After the big project was done,
like everything else corporate,
the vision got diluted
and the hierarchy got rearranged.
Michael was consigned to lesser tasks
like holding swords over battlefields,
greeting saints as they came and went,
standing in for Jesus during the visitation
on an occasional taco.

The Poet Of Dishwashers

In this era of specialization
would our gods get more selective?
Would they save only people
who were left-handed, those people
who were color-blind, those people
who were only four foot two?

I heard a poet called
The Poet of Households
and already I suspect we have become
too selective.
The Poet of Lawnmowers.
The Poet of 8-cylinder engines.
The Poet of People Who Only Have G.E.D.s
The Poet of People Who Like French Roast Coffee.
The Poet of Small Appliances.
The Poet of People Who Like Chocolate.
I suspect that last one would be appealing
to most ethnic and age groups,
but over-all
what would those poets talk about?
What would their message be?

And here is the latest volume from
The Poet of Dishwashers.
Here, just read the cover blurbs.
Do you feel universally included?:

"Best thing dishwashers have seen in a long time."
"I trust this poet's vision, his voice,
his grease-cutting power."
"I was delighted. I was amazed.
I let him scrub my pots."

HALLOWEEN

Casper, Superman, Batman, Peter Pan,
ridiculed presidents
all species of cats, dogs and bears—
and whatever comic character
is in theatres at the time:
they will be waves of them in the neighborhood,
thick as high-fiber cookie dough.

I guarantee you will not find
a poet costume anywhere.
Someone could make one
and give it the title 'Poet'
but the poor urchin would always
have to identify himself.
"How cute! What ARE you?"
                    "I'm a poet."
And the parent at the door
handing out the candy will laugh, maybe nervously.
The poor miniature bard will, of course,
be dragging a wagon-full of rejection slips,
have a flagon of day-old coffee on his hip,
and carrying a pen made from a
dingy white feather.
To complete the look he will need
tattered MFA's poking from his pockets.

At wakes you always wish
you had known the person better.
You find out he had studied
to be an anthropologist,
he grew orchids at his summer house,
had an addiction to kung pao chicken.

Our lives, as we walk through them,
are not as clear and well-stated.
Maybe we should all wear name tags
that state our occupation and desires.
We might feel like centerfolds though.
Perhaps just an indicator
on our driver's license would be better
(since we have no clear idea what we want to be
until we at least get to sixteen anyway).

At parties, bars, social functions, we could just
whip out our neurologist tag
('likes peanut butter and long walks on the beach')
and it would instantly break the ice.
And strip away all pretense.

Instead of waiting for one day a year,
or one final day,
when people discover who we really are,
while we pause there waiting for their approval,
dragging our lives, like an apology, behind us.

Sometimes I Imagine All Reality Is A Ball

but it's my ball.
You might have a pyramid
or a square.
The spatially-challenged might only
have a handkerchief.
But it's really only like
the astronauts
going to the moon.
They always want to
see what's on the dark side.
What is your big box hiding?
What is waiting
on the other side of that hill?
Something grim, austere, foreboding—
or flappy and cartoony with big arrows
and signs for a drive-in?
It's always a future that spins slightly
out of our reach, places we know
we need to visit.
Quick Lube, Great Tacos, Home of the Runza.
Or maybe someone else's
face in the darkness
that our hands don't really know.

No Soliciting

I am going to have a bar installed
on my front door.
You know, the long medieval kind, on a hinge,
or maybe just an old-world beam
that sits on brackets.
Of course, such a system depends on someone
always being home
to lock up after me
when I go off to work.
So maybe I should just add iron plates
to deter hewing axes, Jehovah's witnesses,
and girl scouts selling cookies.
The key, of course, would need to be humongous,
for sheer intimidation purposes.
I would need something much more effective
than a lock on a diary any older sister can pry.
I need to at least have
a sprinkler system for a moat,
or a Chihuahua to substitute
for a spike-encrusted dog.
I need a "No!" that people will believe,
something as clear and undeniable as fate,
something that will repulse even the man
who attaches pizza coupons
to my door with a rubber band.
I want to have an indication so clear
that when I'm old and less able to recall
clever literary retorts
to ward off unknown knocking
that my device or sign or whatever it is
could drive off even Death.
He will read the unwelcome doormat
a letter at a time with his bony finger,

realize I am really serious,
and move on to the neighbor next door
who has high cholesterol anyway.

That Satellite

carries a plaque
with music and words
and pictures of two humans.
It is optimism of the highest cosmic proportion
that that would be all the information
a starry visitor might need
to pique his curiosity.
It might make him at least steer in our direction
and look down on our blue-green ball.
But whoever sent our satellite up
should have considered
that photos are only captured light after all.
When those photos are turned face up,
even something as innocent
as leafing through an album,
or displaying on a screen,
then all those struts upon the stage
will shine up into space
and those all-powerful, light-year-bending aliens
will measure our intelligence
from those billions of photos
shining back up at them,
which will include
my family's faded Christmases,
our starched Easters,
and our summer cookouts
with our mouths dangling hotdogs,
our faces anointed with mustard,
me and my brother wrestling,
my fingers held in a V behind his head.

BON MOT

My mind is not content
with short lines.
Like a description
of a pair
of cardinals
perched around the woodpile
yesterday morning.
No one asked them
if they were related
or married
or simply friends
living together
to cut expenses
to get through
the current economic
downturn.
I have heard
a poem should not contain
a question.
So, declaratively,
I have named
my salt shaker Eunice
and the Pepper Roger.
They knew
my grandparents.
Eunice and Roger
considered divorce once.
They had a big falling out
when Eunice was lost
in the land of stove.
While she was gone
Roger took up
with the sugar bowl,

aptly named Cindy.
But Roger fell one day
and chipped his foot.
There are more stories here
than short lines will allow.

They old ones—they knew suffering.
They needed long lines.
The cardinals forage on
through their sinful state.
Though injured
Roger still keeps
his head held high.

THE FIFTH KIND OF CONFESSION

There are four kinds of confession: talking to God, writing
the sin down, talking to someone else, and the confession
that comes with the passage of time.

There is a fifth kind of confession,
the kind where the sin is passed
through the fingers and lips
onto other objects:
the twisted cup,
the unsettled door,
the catawampus chair,
the gelatin that will not set,
the tea that never gets hot.
I know a beautiful woman
whose eyes hint of secrets
but the last joint of her pinkie finger
has more bumps than a phrenologist
could decipher.
These are subtle errata,
the kind you hope no one notices
but you know, by their very origin,
they must be seen.
It is why the dog barks
at the mower that cuts in patches.
It is the insight of a torn seam
on the black sofa
where you offer your guests to sit.

SCIENTISTS HAVE DISCOVERED CRABS CAN FEEL PAIN

Scientists have discovered
crabs can feel and remember pain.
Does the same hold true
regarding mailboxes on country roads?
Does the soda can
tossed out the car window
feel abandoned
(and frustrated because it has no legs
to find its way home?)
When we first open a box of cookies
do they imprint on us?
There are some things
it is better not knowing.
Sometimes we don't want to carry
so much guilt.

OMPHALOS

This is a place
no one cares about.
No presidents have slept here.
No famous people have stopped by.
It was never threatened by a 100-year flood,
knocked akimbo by a tornado,
or even had a tree fallen on it.
It is simply a room in a rather common house
where I used to smoke a pipe
but through the years
I have evolved to coffee.
The silver cutlery box collects dust.
The cookie jars on the shelves
have not moved for a decade.

Perhaps it is the center of something,
a balance point for something larger.
Some Balinese native walks better right now
because his center, thousands of miles away,
is stable. If I move the napkins he may stumble.

The weight of the sunlight pouring onto
the cushion in the chair the cat likes
is essential for a polar bear
balancing on an ice floe.

Oh, if I spill salt
what calamities! What volcanoes!
I may read of an avalanche,
surprised skiers digging out.

Words like to live here where it is quiet.
They stop by, as sure as fed cattle.

Their ethereal mass maintains things.
They hang from invisible branches,
buoyant in the balance.

If Sophia Loren
decides to stop by
then she can sit in the chair
next to me
as long as she is respectful,
as long as she writes.

FOCAL POINT

Behind the speaker at the conference
there is a wall of movable panels.
If it turns out he is no good
will the wall swallow him up?
A trap door, some summary judgment
propelled by manic applause, or the lack of it?
What do those doors open into?
Another ballroom, another speaker?
Shall we exchange, compare entertainment value?
Is it a mirror-version of us, all books
with author's signatures in the back?
These tiles above our heads,
these seemingly benign vinyl squares below our
feet.
What did Persephone think as she walked
the vernal hills that morning?
Was she only concerned with gathering flowers,
listening to the songs of birds?
Or did she question whether
she had been a good girl,
whether that cracking in the earth
was her fault after all?

FREE T-SHIRT

When the famous writer
came to speak
the venue gave away
commemorative
long-sleeve t-shirts.
Why long-sleeve?
Was he a biter?

When I went to vacation bible school
every summer I would get a little metal button
with a clasp in the back I could bend
so it would hang on my pocket.
And on this button was a picture of Jesus
with his arms around a bunch of children
and the caption said "Jesus love me."

My grandma likes to drink her coffee out
of a mug shaped like a donkey.
From the 1960 election she has told me,
the last Camelot.

This hawking of paraphernalia,
These baseball cards,
These movie posters,
These tears from the saints.
Buddha is coming.
Here is your small box of souvenir rice.
And tomorrow Jesus will be in town.
Here is your free goat-skin bag.
Inside you will find a commemorative crucifix.
Keep it. It might have some value
later.

On Each Tombstone

there should be a forenote.
It should be government mandated.
Something by Dickens, Pound, Thomas Gray,
or some other words
that have outlasted us.
When you are writing your will
it will be gently recommended
you should pick your phrase.
The importance will fall right below
disbursement of funds
and right above
who gets the piano.
If you don't do it
then the relatives will be compelled
to work with the funeral home.
It will be another book for them
to page through
when they are picking the guest register
and type of lining.
"Longer quotes will be more expensive, of course,"
the director will pat your hand soothingly.

Many quotations will become stock, so to speak,
and will be seen over and over,
as common as reincarnation.
Angels will be replaced with ostentatious script.
Large stones, bearing essays, will
be the mark of wealth.

Perhaps it would be best
to be a member
of a less literate family,
forced to used snippets

from the newspaper,
fulfilling the requirement,
regardless of applicability.
"Good machinist available for hire."
"Big train wreck in Chicago."
"Tender Rump Roast. Eighty Cents A Pound."

QUICKENING

I saw him playing in a patch of gray clay
down on the riverbank. He had already made
a dozen gray birds out of clay: rudimentary things,
roly-poly, sticks for legs,
wings outlined with a thumbnail.

I would have guessed he was eight, maybe ten,
and as focused on his task
as if he was reading a comic book.
When I came up to him to watch closer he looked
up to me with the clearest eyes
I have ever seen and said,

"It is exactly as you have always suspected:
It is all about the form."
He made a few more efforts on his latest shape
then sat it down. I saw his lips move,
just a few silent words, then one by one he touched

the head of each clay bird. Like an exhalation,
for each, there was a burst of gray wings,
white flashing, beaks gasping,
then they lifted into the sky, anxious for the air.

The boy smiled, washed his hands
in the flowing water. The strength left my legs.
I sat down on the stones. He straightened up,
walked over to me, leaned in close.

His breath was like roses. He whispered,
"Breathe life into everything.
Isn't that why you're here?"

He looked up into the sky, once, then turned,
and walked downriver, disappearing around a bend.

A mockingbird flew down to the stones beside me.
He tilted one eye up at me and began to sing.

When Cats Walk Upright

The dog was as big as a pony
but when the cornered cat turned
and stood on its hind legs
the dog understood the dynamics
of the whole chasing thing had changed
and now the universe was out of kilter.

The universe is all about balance:
What did that cat have to give up
to learn to walk up tall?

Will he now develop affectations,
a monocle, a cane,
a baseball cap pulled low over his eyes,
a t-shirt that says, "I'm with stupid"?
Instead of running his neck against your ankle
will he now shake hands?
Suddenly he will not have to
look up quite so far
to be disdainful.
But where is his proud profile,
the questing tail,
the secret of hiding behind things
only foot-stool high?
Where is the horizontal stretching,
the total lack of need for pockets?

Did he have to give up the reassuring holiness
of being able to land squarely
on all four feet?

SIGN ON A TRASH CAN

"Temporarily Out of Order Sorry."
I had no idea the universe was so fragile.
I have grown to depend
on the sturdiness of physics
even when I did not include it on
my Christmas card list.
But now, this sign on this trash can
changes everything.
If trash gravity is out of order
It makes me question where previous trash went,
the tossing out of refuse.
the indecision of destination.
Ancient monks would measure time
with a water clock,
striving for precision out of arbitrariness.
They had only a broad and vague notion
of a final brimstone-laden and sin-fed tabulation.
Still, those cloistered people believed
that a bucket measure was always the same
and water would always fall.
So imagine the look of fear on their face
when they came in to check the time
and saw instead an illuminated sign that said,
"Sorry. Clock out of order.
Doom is Coming.
Do you know
where your prayers went?"

Noodling Catfish

The largest danger posed to noodlers are other forms of aquatic life found in catfish holes. Far more dangerous than catfish are alligators, snakes, beavers, muskrats and snapping turtles, who will take over abandoned catfish holes as homes of their own. These animals are always on the mind of experienced noodlers. —Wikipedia

Agnes, at thirteen, learned to tie cherry stems into a knot with her tongue. She was as homely as her name but determined to be popular. She had only a vague notion of what this lingual skill might do for her but at a rudimentary level she had the faith that said happiness followed the smallest of ambitions. The faith of Agnes. It's why we tie words together and then wad them up into syllabic bundles and throw them into the editorial darkness.

Noodling catfish is all about going underwater, full of faith, and then coming up, hair in your eyes, covered in muck, with your hands throbbing. If you get baptized and the preacher's hands start throbbing then he suspects an angelic agent. But with noodling you just don't know what those agents are.

It's a condition we reach for every day. Taking a different route to work, trying a different flavor of coffee, dating a different guy, trying the special of the day, vacationing to a different resort. We weigh out what we are willing to lose. We think we have a sense of where we are going but that's why palm readers get paid—the water's too murky for the rest of us and we're just sticking our hands in holes.

Cousins! Send us photos of nine-fingered Bob!
Agnes, tell us again how many stems you've tied
into knots over the years. You—there—on your
third cup of coffee! Tell me how many words you
have written, how many times you called on the
Muse, and who exactly really showed up.

CLOCKS IN CATHEDRALS

are generally concussive things.
They want to remind you
Doom is impending
and God is watching.
Nursing home clocks are
quiet things
like watches.
Should we get to choose the music
of the events of our lives,
like at a wedding?
Vivaldi, Beethoven, some Gregorian chants?
Perhaps something from Queen
when you wife runs off with her lover?
Something tympanic and menacing
when you get divorced, lose your job?
Perhaps, like poetry, it is all about the sounds
and how we connotate them with what we
say and do and feel.
People in a nursing home
do not want to hear the seconds slipping away.
When the angels visited the shepherds
with the world-changing news
they announced it
with trumpets and a heavenly host.
When succubus come in the night
we want them to whisper.

GUISEPPE VERDI TUSCANO BERTILUCCI

did not do anything particularly great
that we are aware of.
He did not perfect the alchemist stone.
He did not create an exquisite painting technique.
He strode the streets
of Verona unobserved.
He might have come from some bucolic background
and spent his time writing eclogues
that no one read.
He might have worked at a printing press,
a vineyard, a mill, some other smudging job.
He might have been as unique as a sunrise
which today is coming in my window
from a slightly different position
than it did the day before.
Perhaps one day Guiseppe
turned left instead of right,
crossed this bridge instead of that,
misread a Pharmacopoeia,
bought a glass of wine, did not buy a glass of wine.
And tomorrow
the pitcher of flowers on my table
will cast a slighty different shadow
as the sun rises again
in a slightly different position
from the day before
as it rolls and spins and burns
on its glorious, indifferent way.

Before You Disappear

If you're squeamish, don't prod the beach rubble.
—Sappho

you are allowed to look back once.
You always harbored the secret wish
you would be lifted at the last possible second
out of harm's way
and dropped into someone's swaddling arms.
But instead you are drifting, looking down,
bemused and detached.
You know the French have a phrase for it
(and now you know what the phrase is):
the name for things that are left in a person's pocket
after they die.
While you were walking around
the objects were like little moons,
circling in and out of your gravitational sphere.
Now a man is reaching into your pockets,
digging, holding his breath, looking away,
and pulling out the pieces
that no longer have a need to orbit.
He will stir them with his gloved finger,
turn them over, catalog them.
Maybe he will pat your head tenderly,
fold your hands over your chest.
This was not what you expected.
You could have worn better shoes.
Your haircut made you look old.

The only thing that matters really
is moving forward
and leaving all that debris behind.